THE SWAMP

By Pat Birtwistle

Illustrations by Bradley Moore

Patnor Publishing

ACKNOWLEDGMENTS

A heartfelt thanks to Pat Nelson (my friend and research consultant) for her help and encouragement, Nick Sidoti for his enthusiasm, wealth of ideas and insights; Ann Marie Crocco for allowing the students in her school to pilot these novelettes, Angela Marcov who piloted these novelettes and showed such enthusiasm, and to Carole McGregor and Judy Metler for their editing skills. And a special thanks to Paul Dayboll, Linda Roote and Bradley Moore for their help with how to best get these books printed and for creating our website.

Above all, a very special thanks to Norm, my husband and best friend, for all his hard work in making these books become a reality.

THE SWAMP

CHAPTER 1

The Swamp

A hand was there in the mud. On the hand was a ring with a big red rock. By the hand was a locked bag. It was spooky!

The sun was hot, and it was wet in the swamp. The sun hit the bag, and it looked wet in the sand. The hand looked like a stick. Big bugs went up and down the hand.

There was no skin on the hand, but it had a ring on it, and it was like a man's hand would be. No one came into the swamp. Why was it here? The swamp, where the hand was, is big. It is too wet for a lot of things, but it is a hot spot for kids.

The kids' folks did not want them to go there, but the kids liked the swamp. There were a lot of things for kids to do. They did not tell their folks that was where they hung out.

The kids on Nick's block liked to go there too. They went there a lot. It had lots of rocks and hills. The swamp land was a spot for kids, and they had lots of fun in the gaps in the rocks.

The kids looked for things in the sand. Lots of things died in the swamp. They kept looking for stuff.

It was hot, so Nick and Kim went to the swamp. A gap in the rocks looked like a cool spot. They went up and sat down on a rock. Then, Nick looked down and saw it. The hand in the sand. It just looked like a stick. The sun was hitting the red rock on the ring. They had not looked at this spot before and they had not seen the hand.

So, Nick jumped off the rock to look at the hand and bag. Kim did not go with him. She just sat there. When Nick went up to the locked bag, he yelled to Kim. She got up and went down to him. That was when she saw the hand.

They stopped and looked at the bag and the hand. Nick kicked the sand by the hand, but there was just the hand. The rest of the man was not there. They had to think. What should they do?

It was getting cooler now. The sun was getting dim. They had to think of what to do before the sun set.

"Should we get the cops?" asked Kim.

"If we tell them, it could get bad!" said Nick. "What do you think?"

"No! But, what can we do?" Kim asked.

So the kids just went back to the rocks and sat down. Should they tell the rest of the kids on the block? Should they go to the cops?

Nick's mom and dad would get mad if they went to the cops. The kids were not to be in the swamp, and that could be bad for them. Should they just tell Kim's mom and dad? They would not get mad.

At last they got up.

The sun was going to set. The kids had to get back, but they had to think of what they should do. They were in a mess that they could not get out of if they did not tell. They did not want to upset the folks, but the hand could not just be left there. And, what was in that bag?

Now, they just wanted to get out of the swamp. They went back to the block so they would get back before the sun set. All they could think of was what they should do now. Should they tell? Would the hand be there when they went back? Kim wanted the ring with that rock, but she could not think of what to do to get it. What to do? What to do?

CHAPTER 2

Trapped

Nick and Kim were trapped in this mess. They could not think of how to get out of it. When they got back, they did not tell. When Kim went to bed, she could not nod off.

It was just as bad for Nick. All he could think of was the hand and the bag. He would sit up in bed. Then he would get up. Then he would go back to bed. At last, he did nod off.

Next day, Kim met Nick by the swamp just when the sun was up. There was fog, and the rocks were wet and they looked black and odd. Kim and Nick went back to the spot. Would the hand and bag still be there? When they did find them, they wanted to get the lock off the bag but they could not. They wanted to see what was in the bag, and Kim wanted that ring.

"We should look in the gaps in the rocks. We could find things that could help us," said Kim. "This cannot be all there is."

So the kids got up on the rocks. They went from rock to rock looking in the gaps. They kicked the sand. They could see lots of bugs and sticks and things that had died, but not a thing to help them.

Nick slipped on a wet rock. In a flash, a rock slid. A lot of rocks slid down the hill. Kim and Nick hid in a gap in the rocks. The rocks hit the sand. Bam! Bam! Bam! Nick and Kim were trapped in the gap. They could see a little of the sun. The gap, where they were trapped, was little. They could not get out. The rocks blocked them in.

The rocks were big. Nick got next to one big rock. He hit it with his hip. He took out one or two of the little rocks. But the big rocks were stuck! Kim helped him, but they could not get the bigger rocks out. The sun was getting hot, but it was cool in the gap in the rocks.

The bugs did not like the hot sun. One by one they came into the gap. There were lots of bugs, and they were big. The kids saw them. Nick and Kim stopped. They were looking at all the bugs coming into the gap.

A lot of the bugs in the swamp could kill you if they bit you. The kids did not want to get bitten. A bug went up Nick's leg. It was big and black. He wanted to yell, but he did not want to upset Kim.

He hit the bug. It fell to the mud. He looked at Kim. She was still looking at the bugs as they came into the gap. She did not see him hit the bug.

Then a bug landed on Kim's hand.

She let out one yell. Nick hit the bug and it fell. Kim was upset. She let out a yell. Then Nick and Kim yelled and yelled.

"Help!" "Help!" "Help!"

"Why are we yelling?" said Nick. "No one is here."

They were in the swamp. They did not tell the kids where they were going. It was a spot for kids, but not one kid was in the swamp; just Kim and Nick. So they were trapped. At last, they sat and looked at the bugs as they came into the gap. What next?

CHAPTER 3

Help!

Dan went up and down the block. He wanted to find Nick. Nick's mom said that Nick and Kim had left when the sun came up. Dan did not think to go to the swamp. The kids did not like to go there if the sun was not hot. The swamp was too wet then. So Dan could not think of where Nick and Kim could be.

He asked kids he met if they had seen Nick and Kim. They said, "No!" Dan went to see if Kim's mom had seen them. She had not seen Kim. She said Kim left with Nick before she got up. He looked in all the spots where the kids hung out. The last spot he could think of was the swamp.

So Dan went there. He did not think he would find them if they were in the swamp, it was too big for him to find them. Nick and Kim could be in a lot of spots.

Dan yelled, "Nick!" "Kim!" He stopped. Nick or Kim did not yell back. He went to the big rock that the kids liked to sit on, but Kim and Nick were not there. "I did not think that I would find them here. Before I go back to the block to look for them, I should yell again."

Dan yelled, "Nick! Kim!"

Kim and Nick yelled back. "Help!" "Help!"

Dan did not think that they were here. At last, he sat down on the rock to rest. Nick and Kim could see Dan, so they yelled, "Help!" "Help!"

Then Dan said, "What was that?"

He got up, came down from the rock and went to the rocks that had slid down the hill. He yelled, "Nick! Kim!"

Nick and Kim kept yelling, "Help! Help!"

Dan was thinking, "It's them, but where are they? I can't see them." He had come to the rocks where Nick and Kim were trapped. They yelled, "Dan. We're here, Dan. We're in this gap. Help us. We cannot get out. We're trapped. There are lots of bugs in here. Help us. We want water. Help us!"

Dan went up the hill of rocks where they were trapped. "I will see what I can do," he said. Dan got one little rock out. Then, he got one big one out. He was hot from the sun. He had to help Nick and Kim get out. He had to ask them to help him with a big rock. Dan could not get it out. He should go for help. He had to get water. When he said that he would go for help, Kim and Nick yelled, "No, get us out! Get us out!"

Dan did not think that he could do it without help. It was just too much for him.

"I will be back," he said, then ran to find help.

The gap was getting hot. The sun was hitting the rocks and making the gap hotter.

As Dan ran off, Nick sat next to Kim in the hot black spot in the swamp. They did not want to die. But that was what they began to think. If Dan did not get back with help, they would die. They looked at the bugs. The sun hit the bugs as they came into the gap in the rocks.

"We are in for it now. We will die if we don't get some water," Nick said.

"Not if the bugs get us," said Kim.

The bugs went up and down the rocks, but Kim and Nick just sat there. They were not thinking of the bugs now. They were thinking of Dan.

As Dan ran, he was thinking, "What if I cannot get help? What if Kim and Nick die? The rocks are too big to get out, and the bugs could kill them before I get back. They could die too, if they do not get water soon. What a mess!"

CHAPTER 4

The Pact

Beth was at Nick's house. Nick's mom got Beth to go look for Nick to come to lunch. When Beth could not find Nick, Nick's mom was cross. Then she asked Beth if she would go to the swamp to look for Nick. Beth did not want to go. She did not like the swamp. The kids would go there, but Beth was not one of them. She let on to the kids that her mom would get mad if she went into the swamp. She just said that to get out of going. Now she wanted to help Nick's mom, so she went.

Just as she got to the swamp, she met Dan. Dan looked sick. "Get water!" he said to Beth as he sat down on a rock.

Beth ran to get water for him. When she came back with the water, Dan told her that Nick and Kim were trapped.

"Should we get Nick's mom?" asked Beth.

"She will just get upset. Let's get the rest of the kids. We can get Kim and Nick out if we can get a lot of kids to help. The rocks are big, but it will not be too much for a lot of us."

So Dan went up one block, and Beth went down one block. They got all the kids that they could find.

Beth got a jug of water, and they went off into the swamp. They ran as fast as they could to get back to the spot where Nick and Kim were trapped.

When they got to that spot and saw how big the rocks were, they did not think that they could do it.

Dan yelled, "Are you okay in there?"

Nick said, "Yeah, we're okay. Did you find kids to help you?"

"We are here," the kids said, "but we do not think we can get you out. The rocks are too big."

We have to!" said Dan. "If we do not, they will die."

Little by little they helped get the rocks out. Nick and Kim helped, too. They had to stop and rest a lot. At last, they could get them out. A lot of bugs came out, and the kids yelled and ran from that spot. Beth got the water for them. As they were going back to the block, Kim asked Nick, "Should we tell them?"

"Tell us what?" the kids asked.

He did not want to tell them. But, at last, Nick told them about the locked bag and the hand with the ring.

The kids wanted to look for it under the rocks, but the sun was going down. They had to get out of the swamp.

They could come back and find them the next day. They left the swamp. They all said that they would not tell that Kim and Nick had been trapped. They said that they would not tell about the bag and the hand. They would see what they could find the next day when they came back. They would all come to the swamp the next day and look for the hand. That was the pact that the kids made that day.

Nick saw his mom as he came up the block. She was mad, and Nick was going to get it. What should he tell her? If he said that he was trapped, she would tell his dad and then his dad would not let Nick go back to the swamp. He had best just let her be mad and not say where he was.

When Kim got back, her mom said that Dan had come looking for her. Her mom asked Kim if she had lunch with the kids. Kim just said that they had a fun day.

She did not tell her mom that they had been trapped. She wanted to tell her mom, but the kids had made a pact. So Kim just went to watch T.V. and think of what to do next.

Kim still wanted that ring and she wanted to find out what was in the bag.

CHAPTER 5

What To Do?

As the sun came up, Nick got up and left. He took a lunch. If his mom saw him, she would ask him what was up. He wanted to get out and find the kids. They had to think of what they should do. He sat on a rock by the swamp. One by one the kids came and sat with him. They wanted to get going, but they all had to be there before they went back to find the hand. That was the pact that they had made.

When the last of the kids came, they went into the swamp. They went to the spot where Nick and Kim were trapped. They took rocks one by one from the hill of rocks that trapped the kids.

They looked for the hand and bag. They said that the ring with the red rock would make them rich. They wanted to see what was in the bag that could make them rich. They said that the cops would be glad that the kids had helped them if they took the bag to them. They said that they would be on T.V. They had to get the rocks out and find the hand and bag. There were a lot of rocks, but the kids liked looking for the hand and bag, so it was not too bad.

They sat down a lot as they worked. The work made them hot. At last, all the rocks were out of the spot. They did not find the hand or the bag.

The kids looked in the sand. They looked in the mud. All they could find were bugs and sticks and bits of this and that. As the sun got hot, they went to a spot that was not in the sun. They had to find the bag if they wanted to help the cops, and get on TV. They wanted to be rich. They could sell the ring. They had to find the things if they were to be rich.

One of the kids was digging in the sand. He saw what looked like a bag. He yelled, and all the kids came. He dug it out of the sand. "Is this it?" he asked.

The rocks had pushed it down. The kids looked at the bag. It was still locked. They could not get that lock off. They dug in the sand for the hand, but it was not there. The ring was not there. If they were there, the kids could not find them.

"It has to be here," Kim said. "It just has to be."

At last, they got up. Dan got the bag, and they went back to the block. They sat down and were upset that they could not find the hand with the ring.

Then Kim asked, "What should we do now? What will we do with the bag? It looks like a bag from the bank. Do you think it is?"

What the kids wanted to do was to get rid of it. If their moms and dads saw them with the bag, they would want the kids to tell how they got it.

The kids wanted the cops to get the bag. But how could they do that? Beth was the one to get it to the cops. Her mom was a cop. Then the kids had to think of what to do. They would not tell which kids went into the swamp.

Beth did not want the bag. She had not wanted to go to the swamp. Why should she have to do this? The rest of the kids kept asking her. So she took it. She would tell her mom that one of the kids had it. She did not want to tell her what kid it was. She did not want that kid's mom to get mad at that kid. Her Mom was okay with that.

"Where would a kid find a bank bag?" asked her mom.

"The kid did tell me that it was in the swamp, and a hand was next to it," Beth said. "Can we just let it go?"

The next day, the news on TV said that the cops had a bag. A man had robbed a bank and took the bag. The bank was glad that they had the bag back. The bag had things in it that the bank wanted. They said that the kids that took the bag back to the cops did the best thing. Beth took her mom to the spot in the swamp. The cops kept going back to the spot, but they did not find the hand with the ring. The kids kept the pact. They did not tell what they did.

They got into a mess when they went out the next day. That was when they went to the old house.

NEW START SUSPENSE SERIES
BY PATRICIA BIRTWISTLE

THE SWAMP

THE OLD HOUSE

WHAT A DAY

THE JUNKYARD

THE TRIP

AT THE MALL

THE SWAMP

Nick and Kim should not be in the swamp but that is where the kids hang out. One day they find a strange hand with a red ring on it and a locked bag. By the end of the day they get into a big mess.

"I liked this book. I wanted to keep reading and reading."
  -Julian

"The book kept me in suspense."
  -Stewart

ISBN 0-9733663-1-1

www.ingramcontent.com/pod-product-compliance
Lightning Source LLC
Chambersburg PA
CBHW060646030426
42337CB00018B/3474